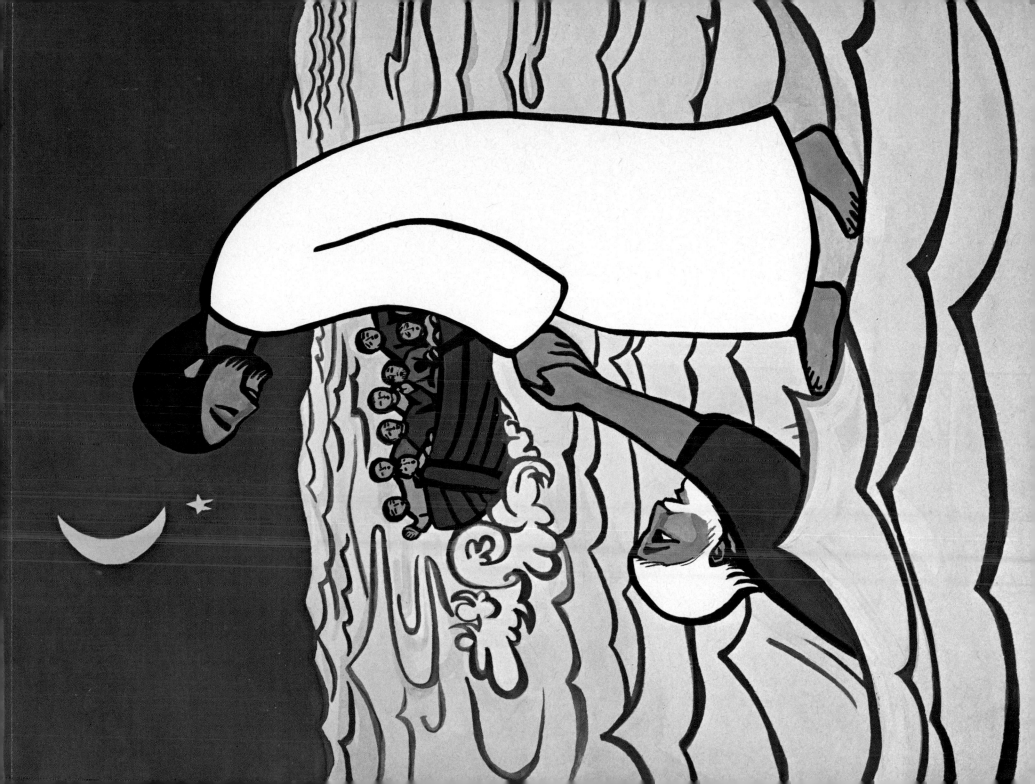

Jean Vanier

I meet JESUS

He tells me "I Love you"

Story of the Love of God
through the Bible-

This book is for you
my brother, my sister.
        It speaks of JESUS and his message
        but it is written especially to help you meet JESUS.
If you want -
stop and spend time with just one picture
one that speaks to your heart and gives you peace
or remain with one text that nourishes your heart.

        If you have difficulties
        share with a friend of JESUS
        he or she can help you a lot
        but especially pray to JESUS
        he will enlighten you.

        Little by little_ it takes time_
        JESUS will reveal to you how much he watches over you
        and loves you

he calls you to follow him
so that you may do something beautiful
with your life and bear much fruit

the world needs you
the Church needs you
JESUS needs you
they need your love and your light.

know, my brother, my sister
that there is a hidden place in your heart
where JESUS lives
this is a deep secret
you are called to live

Let JESUS live in you,
go forward with him!

3

I feel so lonely, unwanted, useless
closed up in myself
such anger and sadness in my heart
disgusted with life and with myself.

One day I meet JESUS
     he looks at me,
     he smiles at me,
     he touches me.
     I can tell he loves me
     just as I am with my difficulties

       my heart rejoices
       a new source of life flows within me
       a small light burns in my heart

Yes, Jesus
    I can tell

    you are really my friend
    you love me and understand me
    you trust me
        and I love you

    From now on, I will never be alone.

And JeSuS guides me
he is my good shepherd
he calls me by my name

and says:

"Be not afraid
in all your difficulties
I am watching over you

trust
for I am with you always
but you must make many efforts
and go forward with me "

" I am leading you to a land of peace and of rest
I am preparing a wonderful feast for you
I nourish you with my Body and my Blood
I nourish you with my heart
I give you new strength
I give you my spirit "

" I love each one of you so much
   that I give my life for you
   I want each one of you to be free and happy "

Jesus brings me into the family of God

He brings me to his father
who is also my father, Daddy

Our Father

so JESUS is my big brother
   I am united to him and to the father
through the Holy Spirit which he gives me
   in baptism.

JeSuS also brings me to
Mary, his Mother
she is also my mother, mommy,
I love her and trust her
she is so much like JeSuS.

18

Jesus brings me into the family of the Father
He gives me new brothers and sisters
in community

I am happy to be part of
the larger family of God now
which is spread throughout the world

that's the Church.

20

And in the family of God
JESUS gives us priests
        they speak of JESUS
        they celebrate Mass, the Eucharist
        they give us the Body of JESUS to eat
        and his Blood to drink

In the name of JESUS they forgive us our sins
they help us live the Good News of JESUS

Jesus teaches me to pray

I look at him
he looks at me

It's so good to be together!
he says: "I love you
as the Father loves me,
remain in my love"

With JESUS I am happy and relaxed.

24

And JESUS says to me:
"When you pray to my Father, say:

My Father, Our Father, daddy!
you are so wonderful, so good, so strong!
Oh, if only everyone could know you
and do what you ask!

May your kingdom come!
May your will be done!

cf Matthew 6,9-13

"Father, I am hungry
        the world is hungry!
            I need you!
            We all need you!
            The world needs you!

Come!
Give us this day
our daily bread!"

"Father, forgive me my sins
     forgive us our sins
     wash all our faults away

     Heal us!"

"Father, protect us
        deliver us from evil
        deliver us from the evil one"

Then JESUS promises me something:

"Whatever you ask the Father
in my Name
he will give it to you
Yes, he will give it to you.
Trust!"

cf John 15, 16

And JESUS looks at Mary, his mother, with tenderness
he says to her:
"Hail, Mary, full of grace"
I pray with him:
"Hail, Mary, full of grace"

Jesus teaches me how to live

JESUS looks at me lovingly
and says: "Come with me, follow me.
        We will live together"

I go with him and I see how he lives:
        He is a friend of the poor
He is so kind and gentle with the lonely ones,
        the little ones, and all unhappy people.

Jesus calls all the poor to him:

"Come to me
all you who are weary and heavy-laden
and I will give you rest
learn from me
for I am meek and humble of heart"

cf Matthew 11,28

40

Jesus gives bread to the hungry

cf Mark 6,41

Everywhere he goes, JESUS speaks of his Father
he always announces the Truth
he is really the Light of the world
he detests what is not true

Jesus comforts the broken-hearted
he loves to live close to them
cf Luke 7,12

JESUS heals the wounded and the sick

cf Luke 5,17

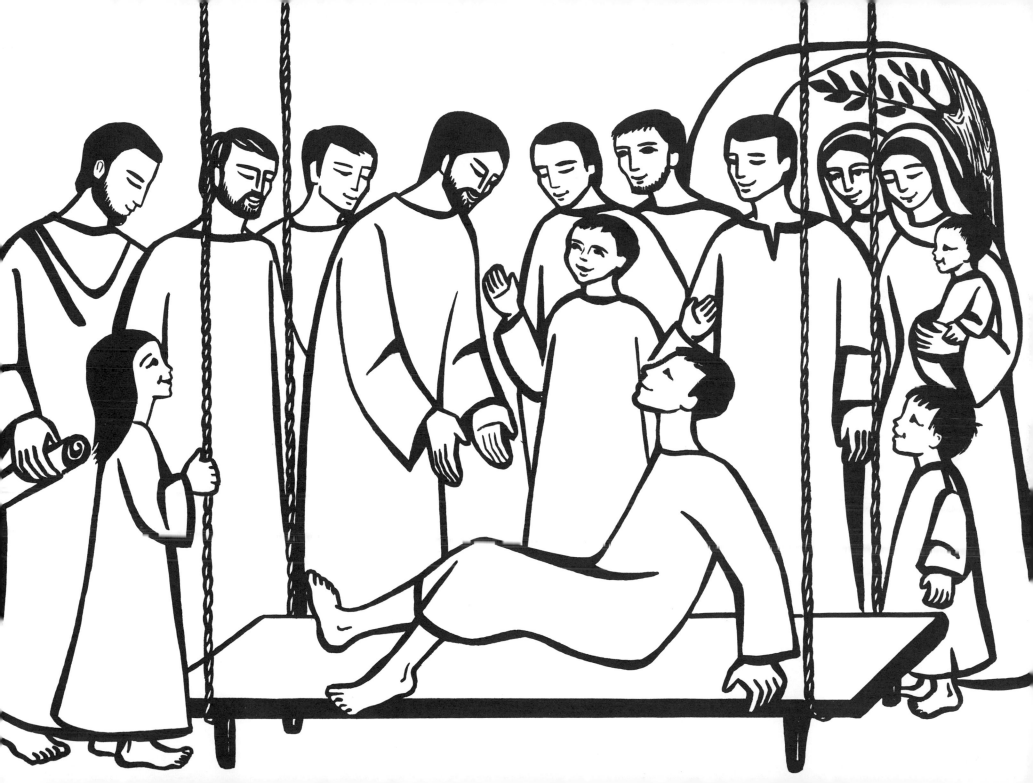

He calls little children to him

he kisses them
he blesses them
because he loves them

he says to me :
"If you do not become like one of these little one.
-full of trust and simplicity,
you cannot enter the Kingdom of Heaven"

cf Matthew 18,2

JESUS tells me a story
     to show how good his Father is
     and how much he forgives us:

  "There is a man who has two sons
     the younger of them asks his father
     for his share of money
     and he leaves on a journey into a distant country.
     There he wastes all his money
                    on loose living"

"Now when he has spent everything,
 famine invades the country
 he has nothing - nothing to eat
 no work
          he feeds the pigs
          but he is so hungry
          he would like to eat the scraps
          that the pigs are eating

          he begins to long for his father's house"

"He decides to go back to his father
        who is waiting for him
        for he still loves his son

When he sees him coming his heart leaps with joy
        he runs to greet him
        he takes him in his arms
        and hugs him

The young son cries and says:
        Daddy, I have sinned against heaven
        and against you. I am sorry, forgive me!

              they embrace each other
              happy to be reconciled."

" the father is so happy to see his son again
that he calls for a big celebration.
Everyone rejoices
the son who was lost, has been found!
he who was dead, has come to life again!

only his older brother is angry
because he is jealous "

cf Luke 15

Jesus why have you come into our world?

JESUS tells me that the Father sends him into the world
to save everyone
reconciling them with him
and making them his beloved children

The Father sends JESUS
        because he loves
        all the men and women
        of the earth

he sends him to announce the good, good news:
        God loves us
        just as we are
we are no longer left alone with our difficulties,
        anguish, handicaps,
everything does not end with death
we are made to live forever
        together with JESUS
and that life begins right now.

The Father sends JESUS
        to free all men and women
        from their prisons of selfishness
                    guilt
                    jealousy
                    oppression
                    violence
                    death
                    evil

Yes, he comes to save us and to free us

The Father sends JESUS
        to be Peace and Reconciliation
        in a world of conflict and war
        to be compassion
        in a world of suffering and misery

JESUS comes to forgive us
        all our faults, our sins
            our cowardice and indifference
    he does not come to judge or to condemn

Jesus comes
        to transform our hearts
        which are selfish and hard
        to teach us to love and to share
        and to build a world that is more just,
        more beautiful, more friendly

                that's the Church!

JeSuS comes
  to invite all men and women
  from all countries and races
  to the great celebration of the Father

  so that all may be ONE in him,
  the King of Love and of Light.

And JESUS looks at me lovingly
        and says:" Be like me
                    filled with kindness
                    be courageous
                    be my hands, my face and my heart
                    as I am the hands, the face and
                    the heart of my Father
    As the Father sent me
    I also send you
                    go announce the good news of Peace
                    tell everyone that God is love
                    liberate hardened hearts
                    forgive as I forgive
                    love as I love
                    struggle against evil as I struggle
                    against evil."

The bishop in the name of JESUS confirms us
for he is the father of the diocese
he sends us forth to announce the good news
and to serve JESUS and our brothers
and sisters, especially the poorest
Through the sacrament of confirmation
we receive a new strength from the Holy Spirit
to be witnesses of JESUS

The bishop also makes new priests

Jesus teaches me his way of life:
the beatitudes

cf Matthew 5

"Live poorly and simply
   do not seek to become rich
   find your security in me
   I am your wealth and your peace

      then you are happy
         and blessed of my Father"

78

"Be gentle and humble of heart
even with those who are unkind
or nasty to you

then you will be happy
and blessed of my Father"

" Do not worry when you suffer
                    when you cry
     I will comfort you
     I will wipe away each one of your tears

     then you will be happy
     and blessed of my Father "

"Thirst and hunger for the kingdom of God,
Yearn that his will be done on earth as it is in heaven
pray and struggle just where you are
for a more friendly world
where the poor are honored

think of those who are suffering far away
and all those who are struggling against evil in the world
pray for them
live for them

then you will be happy
and blessed of my Father"

"Be kind with those who are lonely and rejected
   with those who are sad and in distress
   especially the poorest and the weakest
   share your life with them

   I am hidden in their hearts
   and whatever you do unto them
                  you do unto me
   they will help you
   they will change your heart of stone
                  into a heart of love.

                  then you will be happy
                  and blessed of my Father"

"May your heart be pure and transparent
like spring water

then you will be happy
and blessed of my Father"

"Seek always and everywhere to be peace-makers

then you will be happy
and blessed of my Father"

" If you are kind
   if you love me and try to do what I say
         you will be laughed at
         you will be pushed
         you will be persecuted

               do not worry
               do not be afraid
               I am with you

               then you are happy
               and blessed of my Father "

I say to Jesus

" but it is hard to love, to give
　　　　　to always forgive,
　　　　　to live as you say
I try but I can't
I often fail
so quickly I become discouraged
I become lazy
and just think of myself "

JESUS smiles at me:

" Yes, for you all alone, it is impossible
but nothing is impossible for God
I am here to help you and to forgive you.
        I forgive you through my priests
        in the sacrament of reconciliation
        In that way, you still remain my friend."

"But most important of all,
    eat my Body
    drink my Blood

    So I live in you
    and you live in me

    I give you my heart to love with
    I give you a new strength
        to struggle against evil
        in yourself and in the world "

" Without me, you can do nothing.
        with me, you will bear much fruit.

            but be patient
            remain in my love "

                cf John 15

" If you want to follow me
you will suffer

but be not afraid I am with you always"

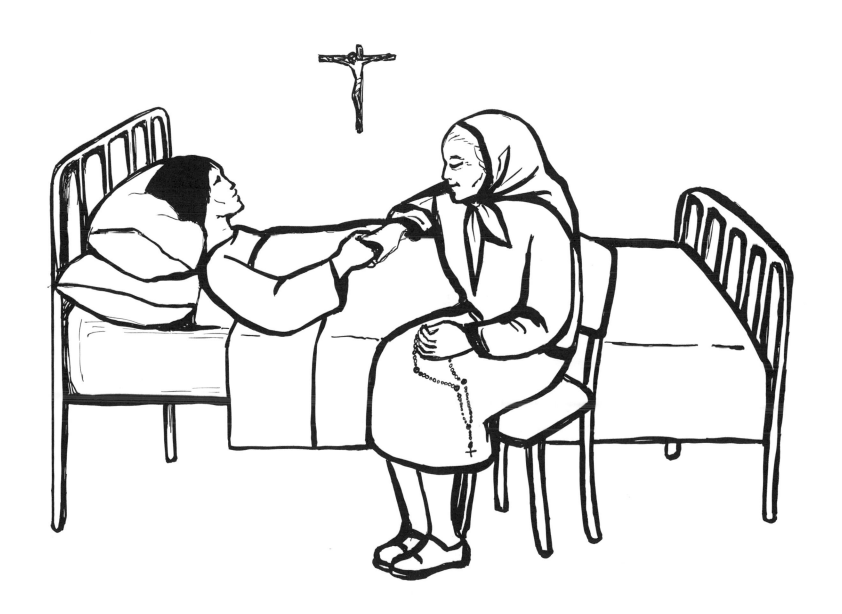

" When you die, I will welcome you forever
into the kingdom of my Father
with Mary, my Mother
and with all the children of my Father

We will live together
we will celebrate together
together we will sing praise to my Father
our hearts full of joy "

" But you must watch and pray,
        for Satan, the evil one
        tries to discourage you
        and to turn you away from me

        But I am with you to protect you;
        remain with me "

" Take refuge in the heart of my Father
        for he loves you

        and watches over you
        you can trust him
        for he is all-powerful in love
                    and tenderness

he knows everything
and not a hair falls from your head
without his knowing it "

And JeSUS tells me:

"The kingdom of my Father
   is like a treasure hidden in a field
   it is worth selling all you have
   in order to buy it "

cf Matthew 13, 44

110

" The kingdom of my Father
is like the smallest of all seeds:
it grows in our hearts
it becomes a tree
where all the birds like to build their nests "

cf Matthew 13, 31

" The kingdom of my Father is like a wedding feast

to which all the poor
are invited ! "

Cf Luke 14,5

Jesus explains the beginnings
and the history of the world

cf Genesis 1

" My Father and I create all things :
      light and sun
      plants, leaves and flowers
      fish, birds and animals "

"But most important of all
we create man and woman

The whole universe is created for them
it is their home and their garden"

" The first man and woman,
Adam and Eve are tempted by the devil
they disobey God
they say to him : " no "
they turn away from his love
then they just look for pleasure in life
they think only of themselves
they no longer wish to serve "

Cf Genesis 3

"And because Adam and Eve turn away from God
and only think of themselves
they begin to fight
and their children do too

And all the men and women of the earth
begin to fight among themselves,
each one just looking for his or her own interests

there is no more love or sharing on earth
everywhere there is war, misery and hatred. "

"But the Father remains faithful to his love
He has a plan for all the men and women of the earth
which is even more beautiful
for he loves them so much
and he wants them to be happy.

He is going to send them a Savior
his only beloved Son
to free their hearts
and to give them new life

and so he prepares his coming."

God chooses Noah
        he tells him to build an ark
        for himself, his family,
        and for all the animals, male and female

And God sends rain, rain, and more rain . . .
        it is a terrible flood !
        the whole earth is covered by water !

Only Noah and his family
        and the animals male and female
        who are in the ark are saved !

And God makes a covenant with Noah
        and with his children
        and with the children of his children
        with all the men and women of the earth
        he will not send another flood
        to destroy the earth.

                        cf Genesis 6

But once again all the men and women of the earth
        turn away from God
        everywhere there is war, misery and hatred.

    God chooses Abraham
            a good and just man.

    with him, his wife and his children
    and the children of his children
    he forms a people, the Jewish people.

    God makes a covenant with them.
                        cf Genesis 15

The Jewish people suffer
    they become slaves, oppressed and humiliated.
    they cry out to God
    reminding him of his covenant.

And God hears the cry of his people
    he chooses Moses
    he sends him to liberate his people.

                cf Exodus 32

After many, many years,
    the Father chooses a young girl
    MARY
    to be the mother of his beloved son

    even before her birth,
    he prepares her for this
    by creating her full of grace
              and love, all pure

she is the immaculate one.

Mary is promised in marriage to Joseph
a good and just man
who always obeys God

The Father sends to Mary a messenger,
   The angel Gabriel
   He greets her :

      "Hail, Mary, full of grace,
       the Lord is with thee"

   He asks her to become
   the Mother of God
   She says "Yes"
      "I am the servant of the Lord
       Do with me what you want" cf Luke 1, 23-38

The Father sends his spirit to Mary
She conceives a little child: this is JESUS
The Blessed Virgin becomes the mother of God.

136

As soon as Mary has the baby JESUS in her
    she goes in haste to her cousin, Elizabeth

Elizabeth is also with child in her old age
Mary goes to help and serve her.

cf Luke 1, 39-56

138

Mary gives birth to JESUS
in a cave in Bethleem

Joseph is there
It is Christmas

shepherds come to adore
the Son of God who has become a little baby

cf Luke 2, 1-20

140

Kings come from afar
to adore him also
and to bring him gifts.

JESUS is king of Israel
king of the whole universe

cf Matthew 2

JeSUS lives with Joseph and Mary
    the simple family life of Nazareth

    he works like everyone else
    he remains there thirty years

After these thirty years
    he leaves his home, his work and his town
    to go and announce to all people
    his message of peace and love :

        the Good News

he also works miracles.

                Cf John 2, 1-12

146

JESUS calls disciples and twelve apostles to join him
he asks them to leave everything and to come and follow him
he chooses them to continue his work
                    to preach as he preaches
                    to be good and kind as he is good and kind
                    to heal as he heals
        among the twelve apostles, there is Peter
        JESUS chooses him to be
                    the rock on which his church is built
                    the first of the apostles
                    the first pope

                    and there is John
                    whom he loves with a special love.

                              cf Matthew 4, 18-22

Today, the pope is like Peter
        he is a friend of JESUS
        the first of the bishops
        the shepherd of shepherds

he confirms the other bishops
he recalls the words of JESUS for all the Church.

Among the disciples of Jesus
there is Mary, his mother.

she is the most attentive and the most silent
she receives his word with love and joy
she keeps all things hidden in her heart
she loves and adores.

There is also Martha and Mary
        the sisters of Lazarus

JESUS loves them very much
        he often goes to their home to rest

cf Luke 10-38

There is a woman who lives a sinful life
JESUS looks at her with tenderness and says

    " I do not condemn you
       go your way ; from now on sin no more ! "

    she will not sin anymore
    for she has met JESUS
    and she knows she is loved infinitely
                                    cf John 8

But others do not want JeSUS
      they are frightened by his message
      they are attached to their money and their power
      they refuse to listen and to welcome his word
      they close their hearts
      they are jealous and try to trap him

On the Thursday before the Passover

JESUS gathers the apostles
to share the meal with them

he knows it is his last meal

Before eating, he washes their feet
and becomes their servant
he says to them:

"Do this to one another"

"then you will be happy and blessed of my Father"

cf John 13

160

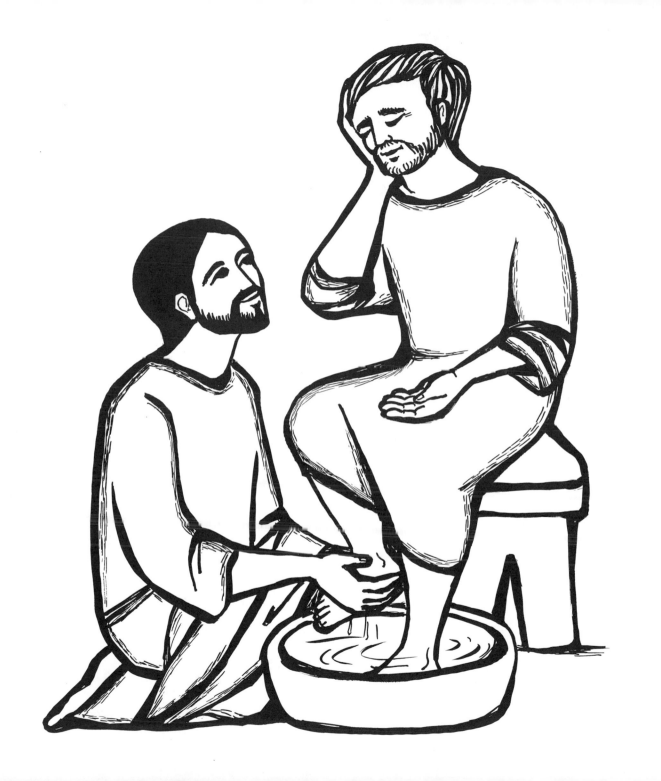

During the meal, JESUS gives to the apostles
his Body to eat in the form of bread
his Blood to drink in the form of wine
a sign of his death and of the gift of his life
it is the first Mass, the Eucharist
He says to them: "Do this in memory of me"
he makes them priests
Then JESUS speaks to them:
"Love one another as I love you
this is a new commandment
soon I will be leaving you
but do not let your hearts be troubled!
I will pray the Father
he will send you the Paraclete
the Holy Spirit
you will be persecuted
but I will be with you always"

cf Matthew 26
John 14. 15-16

162

Then JESUS goes to the Garden of Olives
with Peter, James and John
        he is in deep anguish and distress
        he says to them:
                " my soul is sad unto death "

He prays: " Father, not my will but yours "
                        cf Luke 22, 40

The enemies of JESUS want to kill him
they use Judas
one of the twelve apostles
he comes with soldiers
to arrest and imprison JESUS

Judas betrays him with a kiss

Peter, the first of the apostles, is frightened
he pretends he does not know JESUS
he says:
"I do not know that man!"

and the cock crows . . .

from afar JESUS looks at him with tenderness

Peter weeps bitterly

JESUS forgives

cf Luke 22, 61

Jesus is put into prison
        he is judged
        and condemned to die on a cross
        he is struck
        and crowned with thorns
        he suffers greatly
                    cf John 19

He carries his cross on his shoulders
to Mount Calvary

Simon of Cyrene helps him

JESUS falls a number of times
he suffers terribly

cf Luke 23, 26

The soldiers nail JESUS to the cross
    he is like a lamb - wounded and innocent -
    a victim to save us and to heal us

        From the cross
        JESUS gives Mary to John

        " Here is your mother "

From that moment on, John takes care of Mary
        he loves her as JESUS loves her.

                        Cf John 19

Jesus cries out: "I thirst!"
he gives up his spirit
he dies

a soldier pierces his heart
with a sword
from the wound flows blood and water

cf John 19

They take his body down from the cross
and give him to his mother
she receives him with love

Then they put the body into a tomb
sealed by a large stone.

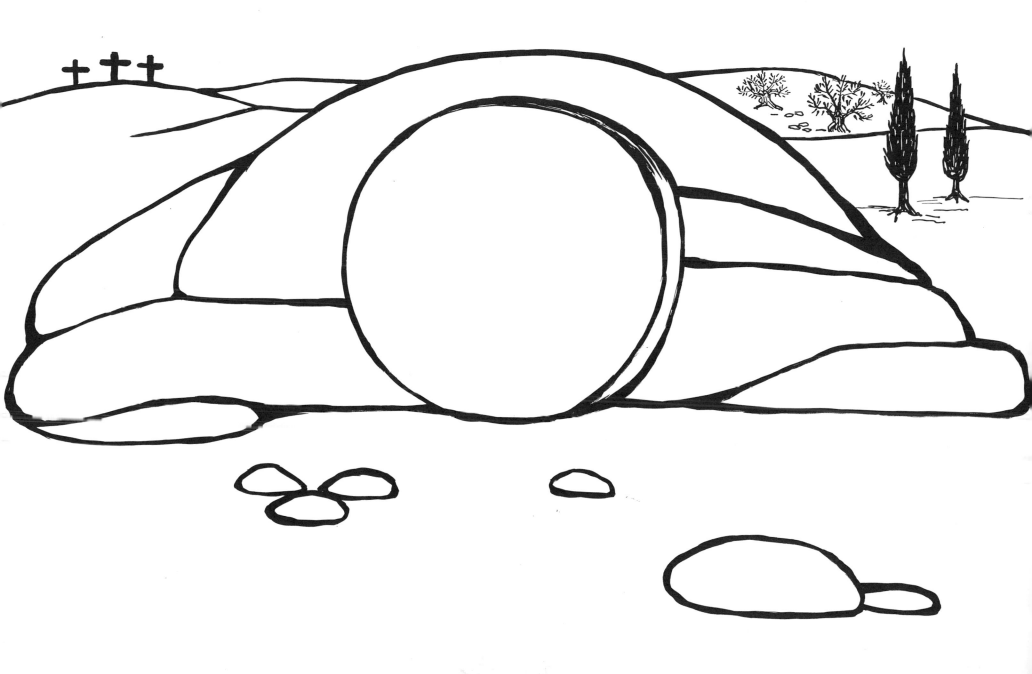

On Easter Sunday

JESUS RISES FROM DEATH!
ALLELUIA!

he is living now and forever!

ALLELUIA!

Early in the morning, Mary of Magdalene goes to the tomb
        she is weeping
Jesus appears to her dressed as a gardener
        she does not recognize him
        until he calls her by her name:
        " Mary "

        she cries:" Rabboni ", " Master "!
        and throws herself at his feet.
                        cf John 20, 11-18

Later JESUS appears to his apostles
at the lake of Tiberias
he has breakfast with them
then he says to Peter:

"Peter, do you love me?"
"Yes, says Peter, you know that I love you"
JESUS says: "feed my lambs"

Thus JESUS confirms Peter
as shepherd of his Church
as the first pope.

cf John 21

186

On the day of the Ascension

JESUS tells the apostles and disciples
to wait and pray
he is going to send them his spirit

Then he leaves them and goes to the Father.

cf Acts 1

On Pentecost Sunday
ten days after the departure of JESUS
Mary and the apostles are together in prayer
they await the promise of JESUS

suddenly, they hear a noise
like a violent wind
and tongues as of fire

appear to them

which rest on each one of them

And they are all filled with the Holy Spirit
a new strength rises up in them
and they begin to proclaim in various languages:

"JESUS is the Son of God, the Savior of the world"

The Church of JESUS is born and is revealed to the world

cf Acts 2

The apostles filled with this new fire
        go off throughout the world
        to speak of JESUS
        and of his good news everywhere
        they baptize all those who believe in JESUS

"In the name of the Father, the Son and the Holy Spirit"

The family of God, the Church, grows in number

Mary lives with John
    John is her priest
    until her death

Then, like JESUS, she rises from the dead
    and enters Heaven with a glorified body

This is the Assumption!

We too will rise with glorified bodies
    at the end of time
JESUS and Mary await us in the kingdom.

The apostles die as martyrs for Jesus
bishops replace them
        they continue to preach Jesus
        and his good news
                throughout the world
                and throughout time

    like the apostles they create
            and confirm christian communities

These communities are made up of
        families - mothers, fathers
            with their children
            and also those who are not married

    some give their lives completely to Jesus

The weak, the sick, the poor, the elderly
     _ all those who are suffering and lonely _
     are at the heart of these communities

they are at the heart of the Church of JESUS

     JESUS loves them with a special love
     he chooses the weak and the little ones
     to confound the strong

Their prayer touches the heart of the Father.

In the history of the Church

JESUS calls men and women
like you and me to be saints
to live the life of the Holy Spirit
        they are friends of JESUS
        friends of the poor
        and our models
they speak of JESUS and to JESUS
they speak to the poor
they are our friends
waiting for us in Heaven.

JESUS is alive
    at the heart of his Church
he remains with us and in us.

    with him we love one another
        we create community
        we learn to forgive and to celebrate
        we welcome the poor
    we give our lives for our brothers and sisters
    and we work towards creating a more friendly world
    we are the face
        the hands and the heart of JESUS

At the heart of our communities
	we pray a lot
	and offer our difficulties and sufferings
	to the Father, in union with JESUS
	so that all the men and women
	of the earth may be saved.

And all together

with all the Church
with all those who suffer and weep

with Mary, mother of the Church
mother of all the men and women of the earth

we await the return of JESUS in his glory

and we cry : " COME LORD JESUS, COME!"

Cf Apocalypse 22

" I thank you, Father
   for having hidden these things
   from the wise and clever,
   and revealed them to little ones "

cf Matthew 11, 25

208